A LIFEGUIDE® BIBLE STUDY

CHRISTIAN VIRTUES

10 Studies
for individuals or groups

Cindy Bunch & Scott Hotaling

With Notes for Leaders

InterVarsity Press

Downers Grove, Illinois

InterVarsity Press® is the book-publishing division of InterVarsity Christian Fellowship®, a student movement active on campus at hundreds of universities, colleges and schools of nursing in the United States of America, and a member movement of the International Fellowship of Evangelical Students. For information about local and regional activities, write Public Relations Dept., InterVarsity Christian Fellowship, 6400 Schroeder Rd., P.O. Box 7895, Madison, WI 53707-7895.

Cover photograph: Dennis Flaherty

ISBN 0-8308-1079-X

Printed in the United States of America ♾

21	20	19	18	17	16	15	14	13	12	11	10	9	8	7	6	5	4	3	2	1
13	12	11	10	09	08	07	06	05	04	03	02	01	00	99	98	97	96			

To Ken "the Commander" DeRuiter

*Thanks for everything you taught
us at InterVarsity Press and
continue to teach us through the
example of your life.*

Contents

Getting the Most
from LifeGuide® Bible Studies

Many of us long to fill our minds and our lives with Scripture. We desire
to be transformed by its message. LifeGuide® Bible Studies are
designed to be an exciting and challenging way to do just that. They
help us to be guided by God's Word in every area of life.

How They Work

LifeGuides have a number of distinctive features. Perhaps the most
important is that they are *inductive* rather than *deductive*. In other
words, they lead us to *discover* what the Bible says rather than simply
telling us what it says.

They are also thought-provoking. They help us to think about the
meaning of the passage so that we can truly understand what the
author is saying. The questions require more than one-word answers.

The studies are personal. Questions expose us to the promises,
assurances, exhortations and challenges of God's Word. They are
designed to allow the Scriptures to renew our minds so that we can
be transformed by the Spirit of God. This is the ultimate goal of all
Bible study.

The studies are versatile. They are designed for student, neighbor-
hood and church groups. They are also effective for individual study.

How They're Put Together

LifeGuides also have a distinctive format. Each study need take no more than forty-five minutes in a group setting or thirty minutes in personal study—unless you choose to take more time.

The studies can be used within a quarter system in a church and fit well in a semester or trimester system on a college campus. If a guide has more than thirteen studies, it is divided into two or occasionally three parts of approximately twelve studies each.

LifeGuides use a workbook format. Space is provided for writing answers to each question. This is ideal for personal study and allows group members to prepare in advance for the discussion.

The studies also contain leader's notes. They show how to lead a group discussion, provide additional background information on certain questions, give helpful tips on group dynamics and suggest ways to deal with problems which may arise during the discussion. With such helps, someone with little or no experience can lead an effective study.

Suggestions for Individual Study

1. As you begin each study, pray that God will help you to understand and apply the passage to your life.

2. Read and reread the assigned Bible passage to familiarize yourself with what the author is saying. In the case of book studies, you may want to read through the entire book prior to the first study. This will give you a helpful overview of its contents.

3. A good modern translation of the Bible, rather than the King James Version or a paraphrase, will give you the most help. The New International Version, the New American Standard Bible and the Revised Standard Version are all recommended. However, the questions in this guide are based on the New International Version.

4. Write your answers in the space provided in the study guide. This will help you to express your understanding of the passage clearly.

5. It might be good to have a Bible dictionary handy. Use it to look up any unfamiliar words, names or places.

Suggestions for Group Study

1. Come to the study prepared. Follow the suggestions for individual study mentioned above. You will find that careful preparation will greatly enrich your time spent in group discussion.

2. Be willing to participate in the discussion. The leader of your group will not be lecturing. Instead, he or she will be encouraging the members of the group to discuss what they have learned from the passage. The leader will be asking the questions that are found in this guide. Plan to share what God has taught you in your individual study.

3. Stick to the passage being studied. Your answers should be based on the verses which are the focus of the discussion and not on outside authorities such as commentaries or speakers. This guide deliberately avoids jumping from book to book or passage to passage. Each study focuses on only one passage. Book studies are generally designed to lead you through the book in the order in which it was written. This will help you follow the author's argument.

4. Be sensitive to the other members of the group. Listen attentively when they share what they have learned. You may be surprised by their insights! Link what you say to the comments of others so the group stays on the topic. Also, be affirming whenever you can. This will encourage some of the more hesitant members of the group to participate.

5. Be careful not to dominate the discussion. We are sometimes so eager to share what we have learned that we leave too little opportunity for others to respond. By all means participate! But allow others to also.

6. Expect God to teach you through the passage being discussed and through the other members of the group. Pray that you will have an enjoyable and profitable time together.

7. If you are the discussion leader, you will find additional suggestions and helpful ideas for each study in the leader's notes. These are found at the back of the guide.

Introducing Christian Virtues

Going to Sunday school was an integral part of Cindy's grandfather's life. From the time Leland Bunch Sr. was five years old until he died just seven months short of the seventy-fifth anniversary of that commitment, he never missed Sunday school.

If Leland was traveling, then he went to the nearest church—Baptist, if possible. For instance, one Sunday during World War II, while flying on military duty with the Red Cross from one post to another, he convinced the helicopter pilot to land the plane so that he could go to Sunday school. The pilot, who hadn't been to church in years, was convinced to go with him.

In later life golfing was Leland's passion. When he was participating in a weekend golf tournament at the local club, Cindy's grandmother would pick him up at the fourth hole, which was next to the highway. She would give him a bow tie, take him to Sunday school and then bring him back to catch up with the rest of the foursome. He would just take an average score for the holes he missed—perhaps surprising a few golfing partners who felt the tournament was more important than a weekly opportunity like Sunday school.

When Leland was hospitalized a few times, his class came to him! Such was the commitment of this Christian community to their time of Bible learning. Members of this class continue to meet together to this day.

Virtues are contagious. People were touched by Leland's commitment throughout his life, and the impact continues since his death. Knowing that their father's last wish in life was to make it to his seventy-fifth Sunday school anniversary, Cindy's father, Fred, and his brother, David, finished out those last seven months of Leland's Sunday school attendance record. Uncle David went to Leland's long-standing class at Fifth Avenue Baptist Church. Fred, living in a different city, attended class and began teaching as well. The discipline of following in Leland Bunch Sr.'s footsteps has renewed their commitment to studying the Bible.

Some might say that Cindy's grandfather was a man typical of his era—persevering, steadily following the same truths of his faith decade after decade—a man who valued qualities that mean little to people today. Even the idea of keeping track of Sunday school attendance may seem quaint, eccentric or legalistic. But he was a man of virtue; he lived consistently with his beliefs.

When we mentioned that we were writing a guide on virtues, one person told us that she didn't think kids were being taught basic manners by their parents. And a teacher recently commented that she sees essential moral values that one would expect to be taught at home being left to the public schools to instill. Though we may be pessimistic about the state of culture, we can be encouraged by the recent success of William Bennett's *Book of Virtues*. The hunger for these classic tales of virtue can be taken as a positive sign. For most of us virtue is attractive. When we find a person we can trust, then that's a person we want to stick with.

The strongest reason to study virtue predates William Bennett's book and even Cindy's grandfather. Long before the bestseller lists began, God set some standards for us, and one of the fruits of knowing him is that he grows us into people of virtue.

What are the virtues God values? Consider, for example, the fruits of the Spirit, the description of love in Romans 12:9-16 and the list in 2 Peter 1:5-6. From these and other biblical passages we have selected a sampling that can serve as groundwork for building a strong Christian character. In studies 1-3, we begin with the inner virtues of faith, hope and love—the essential attitudes out of which all the others arise. Studies 4-10 deal with the actions or outworking of these attitudes: wisdom, justice, forgiveness, courage, moderation, integrity and perseverance.

These are big topics. We will spend our whole lives pursuing each of them in terms of understanding and application. It's our hope that each of these studies will leave you with one new insight about the virtue being discussed and an idea about how it can be enacted in your life.

May God bless your desire to become a person of virtue.

1
Faith

Ephesians 1:11-23

O n our first long train ride, we discovered a very different atmosphere from that on plane trips. Knowing that they would be together for a long trip, passengers were very friendly toward one another. At about four a.m.—to the dismay of Cindy, who wanted to sleep—Scott got into a philosophical discussion with another passenger.

The passenger was from a Muslim background but was searching for a faith of his own. He had read Augustine and Kierkegaard and had lots of questions about their faith. He had done a lot of reading and thinking about ethics as well. Scott and he found common ground as pacifists and prolifers. Scott was impressed by the man's search for truth in terms of both belief and action. And we hope that one day he will find the only true basis for faith—God's work in Jesus Christ. That's the topic of Ephesians 1.

---

1. Is faith something you feel and experience or something you think about and try to understand? Explain.

2. Read Ephesians 1:11-23. According to verses 11-14, what has God done for us?

---

3. What does it mean to be chosen by God (v. 11; see also v. 4)?

---

4. How did the Ephesians respond to God (vv. 13-15)?

---

5. In verse 15 Paul draws a connection between the Ephesians' faith and their love. How does your faith help you to love others?

When have you seen "faith" (Christian or other) that led someone away from loving others?

---

6. What does Paul ask God to do for the Ephesians (vv. 17-19)?

Why would he single out these qualities?

_____

7. How does knowledge of God help make faith real?

_____

8. How has God been revealed to you?

_____

9. When did faith first seem real to you?

_____

10. When are you likely to see faith as something you need to "work on" rather than trusting God to build faith in you?

_____

How can the facts in this passage enable you to escape that trap?

_____

11. Offer your praise to God for the gift of faith.

2
Hope
Psalm 71

Sometimes what we believe about God and what we experience don't quite match. Despite our carefully reasoned theology of suffering, watching the painful death of a family member raises deep questions in us about how God works. Or, even though we know that both the just and the unjust experience worldly blessing, we wonder why God allows the immoral to become so rich. Despite a life of loving God and experiencing God's protection and forgiveness, as an aging man looking toward a menacing future David wondered where God was. Would the God who had been there throughout his life continue to protect him from his enemies? Where could he find hope?

1. What causes you to question God's work in the world or in your own life?

2. Read Psalm 71. In Hebrew this psalm has six stanzas following a five-four-five line pattern. What is the theme of each of the sections:

verses 1-4, 5-8, 9-13, 14-18, 19-21, 22-24?

3. How does David's tone change from stanza to stanza?

4. Which section do you most strongly identify with? Why?

5. What words and images in verses 1-4 reveal David's pleading tone?

6. How has God given David hope throughout his life (vv. 5-8)?

7. What is at the root of David's sense of hopelessness (vv. 9-13, 18)?

8. When have you had similar feelings of hopelessness?

What might be at the root of your hopelessness?

9. What are the sources of David's praise in verses 14-24?

10. Praising God brings a shift in David's mood by the end of these verses. How can praising God bring hope to our lives?

11. Even though circumstances may bring hopelessness, praise God for the things he has done which give you confidence.

3
Love

1 John 3:11-20

Remember the TV show *Love, American Style* from the seventies? One of Cindy's childhood secrets was watching it in reruns on the sly. In the context of that show "sex" would be the essential definition of "love."

How about *Love Boat*, an eighties show? Each week it would end with neatly matched pairs—many who had just met in a shipboard romance. In that show love was often connected to initial attraction. Love was something that could happen in the course of a week. "Infatuation" would be another way to describe this emotion.

How does television in the nineties define "love"? We don't even know of a show that uses the word in its title. For a true picture of love in all its facets, the only reliable source is Scripture.

1. What types of love tend to be overlooked by the media?

2. Read 1 John 3:11-20. What actions and attitudes are contrary to love?

3. What actions and attitudes are signs of love?

4. How does the example of Cain (v. 12) illustrate the effects of jealousy on love between family members?

5. Why would the world hate Christians who show love?

6. How is love defined in verse 16?

7. How have you seen Christians lay down their lives for one another?

8. Why is loving with actions more important than loving with words (vv. 17-18)?

9. How do our acts of love help strengthen our relationship with God (vv. 19-20)?

10. How can you show someone love through your actions?

11. How can you show someone Christ through your love this week?

12. Ask God to help you grow in your knowledge of him so that love will flow out from you.

4
Wisdom

1 Corinthians 1:18-31

$\mathbf{A}$ college student drops his plans to pursue a law degree and goes overseas as a missionary.

A young woman refuses to work the sixteen-hour days that are required to move up the corporate ladder so that she can work with the youth group in her church.

A businessman in his forties leaves his career and moves his family and children to another state to begin seminary.

A retired couple puts their lifetime savings into a Christian bookstore to serve their community.

Each of these are decisions that might be regarded as wise or foolish depending on who you ask. And it is not just non-Christians who disagree about whether these are good decisions—Christians would have different views about them as well. This passage is all about what constitutes wisdom and foolishness.

---

1. When has a person you regarded as wise done something surprisingly foolish?

2. Read 1 Corinthians 1:18-31. In what ways are wisdom and foolishness contrasted in this passage?

3. Why is the cross wisdom to some but foolishness to others (vv. 18, 23-24)?

4. How does God's view of wisdom contrast with the world's view (vv. 19-21)?

5. In what ways do wise people today—many scholars, philosophers, scientists—try to get along without God?

6. What aspect of the world's so-called wisdom has swayed you?

7. Notice the contrast between wisdom and strength (vv. 26-29). What value does social standing have in God's eyes?

8. What does Christ offer us (vv. 24, 30)?

What difference do these gifts make in our lives?

9. What does it mean to boast in the Lord (v. 31)?

10. From this passage how would you define *wisdom?*

11. How can you go about pursuing the wisdom of God?

12. Pray that God will make you wise in his ways.

5
Justice

Isaiah 61

Cindy went to a small urban courtroom to watch her cousin, a prosecutor, at work. The hearing involved a man who had been convicted of manslaughter (killing someone without premeditation) ten years before. As a part of his sentence, he had been ordered to pay restitution of $10,000 to the estate. Monthly payments were set at an amount the defendant could reasonably afford, given his income and expenses. Now, Cindy's cousin said, the ten-year repayment period was up. The law said that his debt could be forgiven. Yet he hadn't fulfilled his obligation because he hadn't paid off the full $10,000.

Although we don't know who was killed or who was left behind, we can assume the family of the deceased person had suffered both emotionally and financially. Was this decision justice for the family? We know that the defendant was twenty at the time he committed the crime. In addition to serving time, he made the payments that were set for him over all those ten years. Was the decision justice for the defendant?

Justice can be a fuzzy issue for us—as it was for Israel. Time and again the prophets reminded the people that an inner attitude of righteousness is not enough. It must show in our lives; we must also be people of just action.

1. What do you think justice means for each of the parties in the opening story?

2. Read Isaiah 61. In verses 1-3 the prophet describes his call to serve. What groups are listed, and in what way do they need justice?

3. What common elements do you see among these groups?

4. What current situations do you know of that fit these categories of need?

5. How would meeting these needs for others be a sign of God's work in you (v. 3)?

6. Because Israel sinned and turned away from God, God allowed them to be conquered. How might verses 4-9 be a source of joy to them?

7. Notice the contrast in verse 8 between what the Lord loves and hates. What do this verse and verses 1-3 tell you about God's concerns?

8. In verses 10-11 the ruler describes God's work in him. What is God doing for him?

9. Compare the actions we are called to in verses 1-3 with the physical appearance of the ruler in verse 10. What is the relationship between right actions (justice) and being a righteous person?

10. Jesus applied Isaiah 61:1-2 to himself (Lk 4:16-21). How does he also fulfill the promise of verse 11?

11. What keeps you from pursuing justice?

---

12. How can this passage be an encouragement to you?

---

13. What actions can you take to bring justice to the needy?

---

14. Pray about the injustice you see around you and around the world. Ask God to teach you how he views justice.

6
Forgiveness
Luke 22:28-34

One day Scott discussed forgiveness in a Christian education class with fifth and sixth graders. One child had just been hurt by another. Name-calling began; voices were raised. There was a real opportunity to try out biblical principles. After addressing this situation, Scott asked the group what it meant to forgive. The child who had been offended said, "Forgiveness is taking someone's sadness and throwing it away." We think that's a great definition of forgiveness. Jesus takes this definition one step further in Luke 22 when he forgives Peter *before* Peter betrays him.

1. What kinds of people and situations are difficult for you to forgive?

2. Read Luke 22:28-34. How would you describe the mood or tone of this dialogue?

3. What remarkable things does Jesus say to the disciples in verses 28-30?

4. How would the disciples have been feeling at this time?

5. In verses 31-32, what is Jesus saying that Simon Peter will experience?

6. How do people today experience "sifting"?

7. Jesus knows that Peter will betray him. How do you respond to that fact in light of Jesus' words to Peter and the other disciples in verses 28-32?

8. What might Jesus have been feeling as he offered his kingdom to those he knew would betray him?

9. Jesus has forgiven Peter before Peter sins against him. What can we learn from his model?

10. How could being open to forgiving others make you a stronger person?

11. Perhaps a person or situation in which you need to offer forgiveness has come to mind. Pray that you will become able to forgive.

7
Courage

Daniel 3

In children's worship Cindy asked the kids to tell about a time when they had experienced fear in facing a situation—when they had said "I can't do that"—and then gotten past their fear. For Bethany it was taking a big leap on the jungle gym. (She demonstrated with chairs, her dress swirling in the air.) For Amanda it was the first day of school and anxiety about whether the other kids would like her.

The times in your life when you are likely to say "No, God, I can't" may be surprisingly similar. It might be an act of physical endurance (giving birth for example!). It might be a big job interview. Or it might be standing up to an unethical client. The courageous choice that Shadrach, Meshach and Abednego made—not to bow down to a secular idol, despite the fact that it could cost them their prestigious jobs in the king's house *or their lives*—is strikingly contemporary.

---

1. What "I can'ts" have you conquered?

2. Read Daniel 3. Describe the characters who play key roles in this story.

3. What seems to be the motivation behind the actions of each character or group of characters?

4. Consider how the actions of each character or group of characters may have changed the outcome. What could have been different results depending on their responses?

5. How might Shadrach, Meshach and Abednego have rationalized bowing down to the idol?

6. When have you felt pressure to bow to the idols of the world?

7. In verses 16-18 Shadrach, Meshach and Abednego speak with theological depth. How do they describe the relationship between our will and God's?

8. What thoughts and feelings do you experience when you read of the fourth person in the furnace (v. 25)?

9. In what ways have you experienced God's comfort in times when you took a step of courage?

10. What has the king learned about God (vv. 25-30)?

11. The courage of the three Hebrew men led to greater honor in God's eyes and in the world (v. 30). Have you seen this result in the lives of Christians you know? Explain.

12. What would be an act of courage that—with God's support—you could take today?

13. Praying together can help us sense God's encouraging presence. Ask someone to pray with you about your need for courage.

8
Moderation

Ecclesiastes 2:1-11

Excess is celebrated around the world. A popular U.S. fashion magazine recently had an article about the most fashion-conscious Russian women. One woman explained that the $300 she spends on one pair of shoes is what a friend earns in a month. Monthly high fashion expenses total from $10,000 to $50,000 for this woman and others. Where the money comes from is never mentioned, but people who do business in Russia tell us that it is most certainly mafia money. It appears that the journalists were more interested in a flashy story than in the business practices of the interviewees.

Magazine articles such as this and TV shows like *Lifestyles of the Rich and Famous* feed the cultural myth that such irresponsible lifestyles are desirable and perhaps even attainable. By comparison, our own lifestyles most likely seem very modest, yet we feed into this myth when we follow the media hype. In the end, as the writer of Ecclesiastes shows, these pursuits are meaningless.

---

1. Give examples of current TV shows, commercials, ad campaigns and so on that promote a lifestyle of excess.

2. Read Ecclesiastes 2:1-11. List the ways in which the speaker has gone about trying to find what is good.

Which of these efforts might be seen as frivolous by popular culture, and which might be seen as valuable endeavors?

3. What clues does the passage give as to why the speaker might have taken on this task?

4. What are some modern-day parallels to the kinds of projects listed in verses 4-6?

In what ways do people try to do the types of things mentioned in verses 7-9?

5. In verses 3 and 9 the writer mentions that "wisdom stayed" with him. What do you think this means?

6. In verse 10 he says that he delighted in his work and this was his reward, yet in verse 11 he says that his work was meaningless.

What important principles about work do these two observations suggest?

7. What does verse 10 suggest about how we find meaning in life?

8. How does the descriptive language in verse 11 illustrate the author's point?

9. What does this passage say about excess?

10. How are you tempted to find meaning in excess?

11. In what ways might you find a lifestyle of moderation more satisfying than a lifestyle that indulges in excess?

12. Pray that you will grow in your desire for the things of God.

9
Integrity
1 Samuel 24

Reno, Nevada. The stark desert landscape contrasts with the garish colors and flashing neon signs of the hotels and casinos. Stepping off the plane on a brief layover, Cindy found travelers feeding the slot machines with coin after coin. The machines made happy whirring and chiming noises. Occasionally the sounds of change jingling down broke in, but the faces of the players were robotic. Posters described the fun that awaited outside the airport—strip clubs, exotic dancers, casinos.

Returning to her seat, Cindy discovered that her wool hat—a birthday present from her parents—was missing. The flight attendants said they hadn't moved it. The man behind her verified that she'd left it there. Apparently it had been stolen. It was a relatively small loss, but disheartening nonetheless. It could have happened anywhere, but we wonder what influence the Reno culture had on the thief's actions. It seemed ironic that Cindy's task en route was to write a Bible study on integrity.

1. When do you find ideas about integrity coming into conflict with life choices?

2. Read 1 Samuel 24. What strong action verbs do you notice in these verses?

3. Taking into account the relationship between David and Saul (see 1 Sam 18 for background), how might one justify the statements David's men make in verse 4?

4. Why does David regret cutting Saul's robe (vv. 5-7)?

5. What small actions of questionable integrity are tempting for you?

6. What do you find surprising about David's actions in verses 8-15?

7. How does integrity involve risk-taking?

8. How do David's words and actions show him to be a man of integrity?

9. How does Saul's response (vv. 16-22) give even more credibility to David's actions?

10. What power does integrity have to turn enemies into friends?

11. What current situation or relationship would you like to change through actions of integrity?

How might you do that?

12. Ask God to reveal the areas of your life in which you need to grow in integrity and to give you friends who will "keep you honest."

10
Perseverance

Philippians 3:7-16

After an accident at work, Lloyd Hotaling (Scott's grandfather) was told that he would never walk again. Yet in time he discovered that he could take a few steps if he leaned on two canes. Every day he would walk as far as he could, moving ever so slowly. Over time, his muscles were restored and he walked without any support.

Perseverance is often regarded as the quality required to reach a goal. When we work hard at something, we keep the expected reward in sight. Yet when we look at our spiritual lives, we know that our central goal—to be like Christ—is one we will never fully achieve in this life. We must continue to move forward, growing in knowledge of Christ and becoming more like him, in confidence that the day will come when we will be made complete in heaven. Paul gives us encouragement and inspiration to persevere in the most important part of life.

1. In what ways have you seen Christians become complacent or discouraged about their spiritual lives?

2. Read Philippians 3:7-16. What words and phrases in this passage characterize us as people in process?

3. What advantages has Paul lost (see vv. 4-6)?

How does Paul's loss help him to gain Christ (vv. 7-9)?

4. How do verses 8-9 define rubbish?

5. What "things" in your life could be considered "rubbish"?

6. Note the things that we are to pursue in verses 10-11. How do these pursuits contrast with the rubbish in our lives?

7. What is a person who is pursuing Christ like (vv. 12, 15)?

8. Verse 13 tells us to forget what is behind and "strain toward what is ahead." Why are both aspects of this instruction important?

Which is more difficult for you? Explain.

9. What has Christ done for you that you would like to "take hold of"?

10. What does it mean to "live up to what we have already attained" (v. 16)?

11. In what area do you need encouragement to press on?

---

12. Tell God of your need for encouragement and your desire to persevere in following him. Allow yourself to receive his reassurance and love.

Leader's Notes

Leading a Bible discussion can be an enjoyable and rewarding experience. But it can also be *scary*—especially if you've never done it before. If this is your feeling, you're in good company. When God asked Moses to lead the Israelites out of Egypt, he replied, "O Lord, please send someone else to do it"! (Ex 4:13).

When Solomon became king of Israel, he felt the task was beyond his abilities. "I am only a little child and do not know how to carry out my duties. . . . who is able to govern this great people of yours?" (1 Kings 3:7, 9).

When God called Jeremiah to be a prophet, he replied, "Ah, Sovereign LORD, . . . I do not know how to speak; I am only a child" (Jer 1:6).

The list goes on. The apostles were "unschooled, ordinary men" (Acts 4:13). Timothy was young, frail and frightened. Paul's "thorn in the flesh" made him feel weak. But God's response to all of his servants—including you—is essentially the same: "My grace is sufficient for you" (2 Cor 12:9). Relax. God helped these people in spite of their weaknesses, and he can help you in spite of your feelings of inadequacy.

There is another reason why you should feel encouraged. Leading a Bible discussion is not difficult if you follow certain guidelines. You don't need to be an expert on the Bible or a trained teacher. The suggestions listed below should enable you to effectively and enjoyably fulfill your role as leader.

Preparing to Lead

1. Ask God to help you understand and apply the passage to your own life. Unless this happens, you will not be prepared to lead others. Pray too for the various members of the group. Ask God to give you an enjoyable and profitable time together studying his Word.

2. As you begin each study, read and reread the assigned Bible passage to familiarize yourself with what the author is saying. In the case of book studies, you may want to read through the entire book prior to the first study. This will give you a helpful overview of its contents.

3. This study guide is based on the New International Version of the Bible. It will help you and the group if you use this translation as the basis for your study and discussion. Encourage others to use the NIV also, but allow them the freedom to use whatever translation they prefer.

4. Carefully work through each question in the study. Spend time in meditation and reflection as you formulate your answers.

5. Write your answers in the space provided in the study guide. This will help you to express your understanding of the passage clearly.

6. It might help you to have a Bible dictionary handy. Use it to look up any unfamiliar words, names or places. (For additional help on how to study a passage, see chapter five of *Leading Bible Discussions*, IVP.)

7. Once you have finished your own study of the passage, familiarize yourself with the leader's notes for the study you are leading. These are designed to help you in several ways. First, they tell you the purpose the study guide author had in mind while writing the study. Take time to think through how the study questions work together to accomplish that purpose. Second, the notes provide you with additional background information or comments on some of the questions. This information can be useful if people have difficulty understanding or answering a question. Third, the leader's notes can alert you to potential problems you may encounter during the study.

8. If you wish to remind yourself of anything mentioned in the leader's notes, make a note to yourself below that question in the study.

Leading the Study

1. Begin the study on time. Unless you are leading an evangelistic Bible study, open with prayer, asking God to help you to understand and apply the passage.

2. Be sure that everyone in your group has a study guide. Encourage them to prepare beforehand for each discussion by working through the questions in the guide.

3. At the beginning of your first time together, explain that these studies are meant to be discussions not lectures. Encourage the members of the group to participate. However, do not put pressure on those who may be hesitant to speak during the first few sessions.

4. Read the introductory paragraph at the beginning of the discussion. This will orient the group to the passage being studied.

5. Read the passage aloud if you are studying one chapter or less. You may choose to do this yourself, or someone else may read if he or she has been asked to do so prior to the study. Longer passages may occasionally be read in parts at different times during the study. Some studies may cover several chapters. In such cases reading aloud would probably take too much time, so the group members should simply read the assigned passages prior to the study.

6. As you begin to ask the questions in the guide, keep several things in mind. First, the questions are designed to be used just as they are written. If you wish, you may simply read them aloud to the group. Or you may prefer to express them in your own words. However, unnecessary rewording of the questions is not recommended.

Second, the questions are intended to guide the group toward understanding and applying the *main idea* of the passage. The author of the guide has stated his or her view of this central idea in the *purpose* of the study in the leader's notes. You should try to understand how the passage expresses this idea and how the study questions work together to lead the group in that direction.

There may be times when it is appropriate to deviate from the study guide. For example, a question may have already been answered. If so, move on to the next question. Or someone may raise an important question not covered in the guide. Take time to discuss it! The important thing is to use discretion. There may be many routes you can travel to reach the goal of the study. But the easiest route is usually the one the author has suggested.

7. Avoid answering your own questions. If necessary, repeat or rephrase them until they are clearly understood. An eager group quickly becomes passive and silent if they think the leader will do most of the talking.

8. Don't be afraid of silence. People may need time to think about the question before formulating their answers.

9. Don't be content with just one answer. Ask, "What do the rest of you think?" or "Anything else?" until several people have given answers to the question.

10. Acknowledge all contributions. Try to be affirming whenever possible. Never reject an answer. If it is clearly wrong, ask, "Which verse led you to that conclusion?" or again, "What do the rest of you think?"

11. Don't expect every answer to be addressed to you, even though this will probably happen at first. As group members become more at ease, they will begin to truly interact with each other. This is one sign of a healthy discussion.

12. Don't be afraid of controversy. It can be very stimulating. If you don't resolve an issue completely, don't be frustrated. Move on and keep it in mind for later. A subsequent study may solve the problem.

13. Stick to the passage under consideration. It should be the source for answering the questions. Discourage the group from unnecessary cross-referencing. Likewise, stick to the subject and avoid going off on tangents.

14. Periodically summarize what the *group* has said about the passage. This helps to draw together the various ideas mentioned and gives continuity to the study. But don't preach.

15. Conclude your time together with conversational prayer. Be sure to ask God's help to apply those things which you learned in the study.

16. End on time.

Many more suggestions and helps are found in *Leading Bible Discussions* (IVP). Reading and studying through that would be well worth your time.

Components of Small Groups

A healthy small group should do more than study the Bible. There are four components you should consider as you structure your time together.

Nurture. Being a part of a small group should be a nurturing and edifying experience. You should grow in your knowledge and love of God and each other. If we are to properly love God, we must know and keep his commandments (Jn 14:15). That is why Bible study should be a foundational part of your small group. But you can be nurtured by other things as well. You can memorize Scripture, read and discuss a book, or occasionally listen to a tape of a good speaker.

Community. Most people have a need for close friendships. Your small group can be an excellent place to cultivate such relationships. Allow time for informal interaction before and after the study. Have a time of sharing during the meeting. Do fun things together as a group, such as a potluck supper or a picnic. Have someone bring refreshments to the meeting. Be creative!

Worship. A portion of your time together can be spent in worship and prayer. Praise God together for who he is. Thank him for what he has done and is doing in your lives and in the world. Pray for each other's needs. Ask God to help you to apply what you have learned. Sing hymns together.

Mission. Many small groups decide to work together in some form of outreach. This can be a practical way of applying what you have learned. You can host a series of evangelistic discussions for your friends or neighbors. You can visit people at a home for the elderly. Help a widow with cleaning or repair jobs around her home. Such projects can have a transforming influence on your group.

For a detailed discussion of the nature and function of small groups, read *Small Group Leaders' Handbook* or *The Big Book on Small Groups* (both from IVP).

Study 1. Faith. Ephesians 1:11-23.

Purpose: To see faith as based in the Person we believe in rather than our own strength.

Background. This book was written to encourage the churches in Asia Minor and around Ephesus to continue Paul's mission. In these verses the readers are called to remember their salvation.

Question 1. Every study begins with an "approach" question, which is meant to be asked before the passage is read. These questions are important for several reasons.

First, they help the group to warm up to each other. No matter how well members of a group may know each other, there is always a stiffness that needs to be overcome before people will begin to talk openly. A good question will break the ice.

Second, approach questions get people thinking along the lines of the topic of the study. Most people will have lots of different things going on in their minds (dinner, an important meeting coming up, how to get the car fixed) that have nothing to do with the study. A creative question will get their attention and draw them into the discussion.

Third, approach questions can reveal where our thoughts or feelings need to be transformed by Scripture. That is why it is especially important not to read the passage before the approach question is asked. The passage will tend to color the honest reactions people would otherwise give because they are, of course, supposed to think the way the Bible does. Giving honest responses before they find out what the Bible says may help them see where their thoughts or attitudes need to be changed.

Most of us will have some understanding and experience of both the feeling and thinking aspects of faith, but our personalities tend to push us more strongly in one direction or the other.

Question 2. These verses can be seen as a brief summary of the gospel. Note that each person of the Trinity is mentioned.

Question 3. Some will read these verses as saying that we are all chosen to be with God, and others will read them as speaking of the predestination of the elect few. Here's how Andrew T. Lincoln puts it:

"This clause heavily underlines that believers' appointment in Christ to their destiny is part of God's sovereign purpose. . . . with the description of God as the one who carries out or works all things according to his own will" (*Ephesians* [Waco, Tex.: Word, 1990], p. 36).

Members of your group may disagree about what the implications are for all people, but Christians of either conviction can revel in the miracle of grace that has been extended.

Question 5. Sometimes immature, overzealous faith can alienate those we want to win over to Christ, especially family members. Mature faith perseveres in love even when the other person ignores or rejects the gospel. Other examples would include Muslim fundamentalists who use violence or those in cultic groups who emphasize certain practices more than faith in Christ.

Question 6. Andrew Lincoln offers the following insight: "In the O.T., wisdom often involves practical knowledge, the ability to choose right conduct, while in Paul it often involves understanding God's activity in Christ and the benefits it brings to believers" (*Ephesians,* pp. 56-57).

Question 7. Some Christian groups tend to emphasize faith and others experience, but verses 17-20 show how the two are intertwined: knowledge brings a deep inner experience of faith.

Question 9. If you have seekers in your group, you could rephrase this to say, "What indications do you have that faith is real?"

Question 10. This passage draws us to see that our faith is true because of who Christ is and not because of how strongly we believe. These verses call us away from self-sufficient behavior, such as trying harder to believe certain truths, studying more or praying more, that takes the focus off Christ.

Between studies. To help integrate the virtues as you go along, encourage group members to consider the following questions each week between meetings: (1) Which virtue have you had an opportunity to exercise this week? (2) Which virtue has been a struggle for you and why? Then follow up at the beginning or end of each study and discuss your progress in making these virtues a part of your lives.

Study 2. Hope. Psalm 71.

Purpose: To show how hopelessness results from focusing inward, while keeping the focus on God restores hope.

Question 2. *The NIV Study Bible* points out the confident expression of hope at the center of the passage (vv. 14-16) "framed by an appeal for help" (vv. 1-4) and a vow to praise in anticipation of deliverance (vv. 22-24). The second and fifth stanzas have references to times of trouble (v. 7—"like a portent"— and v. 20). Stanzas three and four point out that the king is aging.

Question 3. David seems to move back and forth from declaring his hope in the Lord to presenting his plea for help, for example in verse 1 and between verses 8 and 9. It seems that by recalling how God has been faithful to him in the past (v. 17) David is reminding himself that he can be confident about his future (vv. 20-21).

Question 6. Because this psalm was evidently written late in life, David has the luxury of looking back to see what God has done for him over the years. Verses 5 and 6 show that David recognizes God's hand guiding him throughout his life. Verse 7 refers to David as a "portent." This could mean either that (1) David was seen as a shining example of God's care or that (2) David was seen as one who had received God's judgment. Either would make sense in David's life, but in each case David recognizes that it is God who has protected him even when he did not deserve it. (Marvin E. Tate, *Psalms 51—100* [Waco, Tex.: Word, 1990], p. 214)

Question 7. A couple of factors likely come into play here: David is aging and seems to fear the weakness that comes with old age (vv. 9, 18), and David still has enemies who pursue him (vv. 4, 10, 24).

Question 9. In verses 14-24 David praises God for his loving actions in the past and also for what David *expects* God to do in the future.

Question 10. In the process of offering his praise to God, David recalls how good God is, and that gives him greater confidence about his own future.

Question 11. If time allows, you can discuss how God is currently encouraging you, or you can make this the subject of closing prayer.

Study 3. Love. 1 John 3:11-20.

Purpose: To see how love grows out of putting our faith and hope in Christ.

Question 1. Help the group to think of a variety of relationships that require some type of love to be healthy. Friendships and family, for example, are important areas of life that need love as much as the sexual/romantic love usually featured in the media.

On *Seinfeld* the commitment between friends seems dependent on the amusement they provide one another. One senses that Jerry is unlikely to make a major—and only rarely a minor—sacrifice for George, Elaine or Kramer. *Friends* makes a significant contribution by showing caring *friendships,* but the characters generally seem to float from one *romantic* relationship to the next, having little interest in sticking with one person.

Question 4. Cain's story is told in Genesis 4:1-12.

Question 5. The thought in verse 13 echoes the words of Jesus in John 15:18-19. This verse is connected to verse 12, where Cain's actions were explained as resulting from a realization that Abel's actions were more righteous. When Christians show their love, the world is forced to recognize its own unrighteousness. Note also that verse 13 is sometimes translated "that the world hates you" (NRSV) or "when the world hates you" (*The Message*), implying that when Christians love as Jesus has commanded, the world will necessarily respond negatively.

Question 7. Though we may not literally be called to lay down our lives, we can give up our own interests for the sake of others in many small ways at work and at home. A more direct parallel comes from the lives of the parents of an eight-year-old child who died. In the midst of their grief and the need to make decisions about burial and so on, they made the choice to give the liver of their son to a ten-month-old baby in need of a transplant. Both families are Christian.

Another example of sacrifice comes from college chaplain Tim Dearborn. Injured in a boating accident in Alaska, Dearborn needed blood transfusions. Because there was no blood bank in the town, an appeal for donors went out on the radio.

"Weeks after my discharge from the hospital . . . I was taking my first walk down the main street of the town. Life seemed so full and good. The air smelled purer; the sea gulls and even the ravens sounded more melodious. . . . The pharmacist emerged from his store. I'd never met him before, but he called me by name. He asked me how I was feeling and then said, 'Praise God that you've recovered. You better take good care of yourself. I've a pint of my blood invested in you.'

"My very life had become for him an icon. His blood given for me—a physical reminder of Christ's blood given for us" (*Taste & See* [Downers Grove, Ill.: InterVarsity Press, 1996], p. 82).

Question 9. In the presence of a holy God we become aware of the sin in our hearts. Verses 19-20 seem to assume that we will have a certain "guilty conscience" when we are before God. However, reassurance is offered that if we love "with actions and in truth," then we can be sure that God will accept us, regardless of how unworthy we feel.

Verse 19 may be translated with the future tense "we shall know," according to one translator, and perhaps suggests a crisis in which we will need reassurance, rather than implying a constant certainty that we are "on God's side." So this may be referring to a final sort of judgment or to God's ongoing judgment. In verse 20, while divine judgment is not excluded, John's main purpose is to "reassure his readers that when believers are most aware of their shortcomings in respect of God's standards, the love and mercy of the Father are present to heal their troubled consciences" (Stephen S. Smalley, *1, 2, 3 John* [Waco, Tex.: Word, 1984], p. 203).

Questions 10-11. As these questions are discussed, the leader needs to model vulnerability by responding to them with specific honest comments.

Study 4. Wisdom. 1 Corinthians 1:18-31.

Purpose: To look at wisdom in light of the cross rather than in light of the world.

Question 2. Help the group begin to recognize the different meanings Paul gives to *wisdom* and *foolishness* in this passage. Paul is using a form of irony in this passage; group members may miss it if they aren't looking for it. It may be helpful to insert "so-called" before the references to wisdom and wise people in verse 20. Also, note that verse 19 is a reference to Isaiah 29:14, where God promises to turn the religious expectations of Israel upside down.

Question 3. Be sure that the group picks up on God's role in helping us to see the wisdom of the cross—and that they also recognize the role of faith in understanding the cross.

Question 4. Again note Paul's tone in the passage. Also, discuss the ways in which God's view turns everything upside down and completely alters our understanding of the world.

Question 5. This question is not intended to begin a lengthy debate about the relative merits of secular learning. Rather, it is intended to help us think about how we may sometimes leave God in the church while we go about our weekday lives with the same worldview as the secular world. This may mean we are putting our faith in things considered wise by the world but not considered so by God.

Question 9. This verse refers to Jeremiah 9:23-24, another passage about how the wise, strong and rich need to boast about their understanding of God instead of about their wisdom, strength or wealth. For those who are fascinated with the idea of boasting, see also 2 Corinthians 11 where Paul does a little boasting of his own.

Study 5. Justice. Isaiah 61.

Purpose: To learn about how the Lord regards justice and how we can become people who practice justice.

Question 1. Don't allow this question to derail your group into a lengthy political and social debate. An alternate opening question would be "Who in your community needs justice?"

Question 2. There are many similar passages in which the prophets call the people to justice and describe how God blesses just actions. See, for example, Micah 3.

Jesus quoted verses 1 and 2 in reference to himself (Lk 4:16-21). According to *The NIV Study Bible,* verse 1 "may refer to Isaiah in a limited sense, but the Messianic servant is the main figure intended" (Kenneth Barker, ed.

[Grand Rapids, Mich.: Zondervan, 1985], p. 1106).

The events in these verses are comparable to those in the Year of Jubilee (Lev 25) when debts were to be forgiven, slaves released and land returned to its original owners.

Question 3. These are voiceless people—children, women, prisoners—and the oppressed—slaves, the poor.

Question 4. Consider groups of people and personal acquaintances such as abuse victims, those in poverty, prisoners and victims of war.

Question 5. According to John D. W. Watts, "The chapter contains a balanced picture of ministries for God's peoples. The spirit-anointed preacher of good news to the disadvantaged and oppressed continues the role of the suffering one of 50:4-9 and 52:13—53:12. He is God's direct line of communication to the outsiders, the needy and distressed" (*Isaiah 34—66* [Word: Waco, Tex., 1987], p. 305). In Luke's Gospel, Jesus emphasizes that he has come for *all* people, not just the rich and powerful. These are the people to whom God wants us to demonstrate his love.

Question 6. In verses 4-7 and 10-11, Watts suggests that we have a new speaker, an administrator or ruler. The speaker may be Artaxerxes (Ezra 7:12-29). These verses would refer to "his success in stabilizing his regime and in winning full control of Palestine" (*Isaiah 34—66*, p. 304). Others feel that it is the prophet or "Anointed One" whose voice continues throughout this passage (see J. Alec Motyer, *The Prophecy of Isaiah* [Downers Grove, Ill.: InterVarsity Press, 1993], pp.499-505). Note also that in verses 8-9 the speaker is Yahweh.

Question 7. Throughout Scripture we see God's concern for voiceless people. For example, in Deuteronomy 10:18 we are told to defend orphans and widows and give help to aliens. Psalm 10 reminds us to care for the helpless (v. 12) and mentions "the fatherless and the oppressed" (vv. 17-18). Jesus refers to the Isaiah passage in Luke 4:17-19 as well.

Study 6. Forgiveness. Luke 22:28-34.

Purpose: To understand that in the knowledge that Jesus forgives us, we are freed to forgive others.

Background. This exchange takes place at the Last Supper. Jesus is still struggling with his coming death; later in the chapter he prays for a way out. In verses 14-20 Jesus offers them the bread and the wine—saying that they are his body and blood. Yet, in the very next verses (24-27) the disciples get into a dispute about who is the greatest.

Question 5. It is interesting to note that in verse 31 Jesus tells Peter that

Satan has asked permission "to sift you-all", that is, all of the disciples, not just Peter. The image of sifting is agricultural, and would have been familiar to both Peter and the readers of Luke's Gospel. Wheat was sifted in order to separate the valuable grain from the worthless chaff. However, Jesus has prayed for Peter that his betrayal will not be complete.

Question 6. You may recall Job 1:6-12 where God allows Satan to test Job to see if he will remain faithful. God's requirement is that Satan preserve Job's life. This passage confirms that temptation, though allowed by God, doesn't come from God (Jas 1:13).

Question 7. At the height of the disciples' selfishness and in full view of their coming tragic weakness, Jesus offers precisely what they are asking for (vv. 32, 34), though they can hardly understand it yet. This demonstrates Jesus' ability to forgive on a very personal level.

Question 8. Here, as in the rest of the passage, we should not allow the foolishness of the disciples to keep us from noticing how we are like them. We too betray Jesus. If appropriate, you might discuss this as a group.

Study 7. Courage. Daniel 3.

Purpose: To provide encouragement for Christians to maintain their unique identity even in a hostile environment.

Question 2. List details about Nebuchadnezzar, the astrologers, and Shadrach, Meshach and Abednego in this and the next two questions.

More background on Shadrach, Meshach and Abednego and their relationship with Nebuchadnezzar can be found in Daniel 1—2. They would have been part of the group of officials mentioned in verse 3 because the king had made them advisors in 2:49.

Question 4. It is encouraging to note that the ungodly actions on the part of Nebuchadnezzar and the astrologers led to God's being glorified by Shadrach, Meshach and Abednego.

Question 5. One way of looking at it might be to say that they should make use of their place of power and influence: Perhaps if they would bow down now, they could later develop a stronger relationship with the king and gradually influence him to see their way. This is the sort of approach we take when we assume we can shape our own futures better than God can.

Question 6. Depending on the group's response, a possible follow-up question would be, "When is it tempting for you to bypass one of God's commands?"

Question 7. They fully believe that God can rescue them (v. 17), yet they acknowledge that he may not (v. 18). They tell the king that either way they will follow God's commands.

Question 8. Psalm 91:9-16 promises that God commands his angels to guard those who love him and "acknowledge" his name. According to the *New Bible Commentary:* "Early Christian commentators viewed the fourth figure as an appearance of the Son of God or as the angel of the Lord (see v. 28) and have been frequently followed. The emphasis, however, is on the completeness of God's protection shown by the fact that they emerged without even the *smell of fire on them* (27)" (G. J. Wenham, ed., *New Bible Commentary: 21st Century Edition* [Downers Grove, Ill.: InterVarsity Press, 1994] p. 752). We can take this verse as an example of how God offers us comfort and encouragement through the hard times.

Question 10. The king moves from referring to the fourth person as "a son of the gods" (v. 25)—a pagan reference—to calling the man "an angel" (v. 28). He refers to their God as "the Most High God" (v. 26). He knows that "no other god can save." And he realizes that those who trust in God can be trusted by him (v. 30).

Question 11. Many may feel that worldly honor for being faithful to God is not a typical experience for Christians today. Yet perhaps you can think of examples in your community in which people who are honest in business and professional work are well thought of. It takes great courage to stand apart from accepted gray areas where corners are cut and morals are questionable. Many Christians on university campuses and in other settings are pressured to uphold "tolerance" as the highest value while New Age practices and other religions are embraced.

Study 8. Moderation. Ecclesiastes 2:1-11.

Purpose: To expose cultural myths about excess as a source of meaning in life and to discover how to find satisfaction in moderation.

Question 1. You might also encourage the group to explore the implicit values and meaning that are communicated along with the "worldly" lifestyle. Also encourage people to think of not just the most outrageous examples, but of some that affect them.

If you prefer, you might simply ask, "Where have you observed excesses in lifestyle?"

Question 2. Be sure that the group notes both the *types* of endeavors made by the speaker and their *scope*. For example, he not only owned livestock, but also "more herds and flocks than anyone in Jerusalem before me."

The author of Ecclesiastes is never named in the text. Many people have noted that the experiences related in the book sound very much like what we know of King Solomon. This is especially true in the passage used for this study. However, it could have been a later writer with similar experiences or even someone writing from Solomon's perspective.

It is also interesting to note that Ecclesiastes names God only once. This is a very secular struggle on the part of the writer, yet we know that God is in the background of his life.

Question 3. The book of Ecclesiastes is itself primarily hindsight commentary and analysis from one who has struggled to find meaning and true profit from what life has to offer. These verses reveal part of that struggle and search as the author tries to find meaning and value in pleasure. It is important to remember that the various activities were pursued not for their own sake but so that the author could find some ultimate meaning. In many ways, then, the author of Ecclesiastes can be seen as someone who is very contemporary. Many people today look to various activities to give their lives meaning.

Question 6. These questions may lead you into a discussion about the meaning of work. Compare the biblical statements to some common assumptions we make today about work. For example, when someone asks "What do you do?" they usually expect to hear what your job is. Or talk about the ways in which we categorize those whose job status is less than we think it should be.

Question 10. Consider not just the areas of life in which you are tempted to excess, but also what sorts of activities and events lead you into that temptation.

Question 11. It may be helpful to talk in the group about what a lifestyle of excess looks like. There are at least two ways to think of excess. One is to look at how much we have or do in a certain area of life. Another is to look at the contrast between what we have and do and what is actually necessary. A lifestyle of moderation can likewise be seen as how little we have and do. Or we can look at how closely what we have and do matches what we actually need.

Study 9. Integrity. 1 Samuel 24.

Purpose: To discover how our character and our relationships are affected when we are people of integrity.

Question 1. You might get at this question by focusing on various subgroups in people's lives—extended family, church, work.

Question 2. There are powerful verbs throughout this passage, for example: crept, cut off, rebuked, attack, bowed, prostrated, delivered, urged, kill, spared, understand, recognize, hunting, avenge.

Question 3. Saul had become jealous of David (1 Sam 18) because of his popularity with the people. In 1 Samuel 18:28-29 we read that Saul became David's enemy because he realized the Lord was with David (see also 18:12). Saul had been pursuing David and trying to kill him. David and his men (1 Sam 22:2 says there were 400 men, though we don't know exactly how many were in the cave) were hiding from Saul.

Question 4. We see in the text David's great respect for "the LORD's anointed." This is further emphasized by 1 Samuel 26:9-11, a similar account. According to the Word Biblical Commentary *1 Samuel* by Ralph W. Klein (Waco, Tex.: Word, 1983), p. 239, David's cutting of Saul's robe echoes 15:27 in which Saul tore Samuel's robe. It could be read as a sign that the kingdom would be torn from Saul (see, for example, 1 Kings 11:29-31). If so, then that would explain David's reaction. Possession of even part of the royal robe might imply that David was "the legitimate heir" (see 1 Sam 18:4). Later in the passage (v. 12), David shows the piece as a sign of his innocence, bypassing a chance to take Saul's life.

Question 7. In the text David takes a big risk by showing himself to Saul and acknowledging what he has done. Move from the biblical example to how this connects to life today.

Study 10. Perseverance. Philippians 3:7-16.

Purpose: To inspire us to continue on in knowing Christ, looking toward the day we will be in heaven with him.

Question 3. The verses previous to our study passage contain a list of the various advantages that Paul had either inherited or achieved in his life before he encountered Jesus on the road to Damascus (Acts 9). As a Jew attempting to merit God's favor, Paul's accomplishments were considerable. However, those achievements were themselves keeping him from seeing his need for salvation through Jesus. He could not continue to put his faith in his own accomplishments and also put his faith in Jesus.

Question 4. Paul's use of *rubbish* should be seen not only as a comparison between what we have without Jesus and what Jesus offers us. It is also a condemnation of those things which give us false hope in ourselves and make us act as if we don't really need God's gifts.

Question 5. Help the group to keep in mind that this entire section is very autobiographical. Paul is speaking of the things in his life that kept him from Jesus. Those very things could have been helpful to someone else. It would be a mistake to think that each person would struggle with the same issues. For example, some people find that theological education helps them to know and understand God better, while for others it only increases their tendencies toward self-sufficiency. The important issue is for each person to be able to identify what keeps them from being dependent on God's grace alone.

Question 6. When we are pursuing Christ, many things that seemed important and absorbed much of our time and energy—reaching a goal at work, getting the house in order, buying a new car before the old one falls apart—pale in comparison. This does not mean that we should be irresponsible in our earthly responsibilities, but that we should always measure our lives by our growth in knowing Christ.

Some group members may wonder at Paul's choice of words about the resurrection in verse 11. For Paul, "the resurrection is certain; the intervening events are uncertain," according to J. A. Motyer (*The Message of Philippians* [Downers Grove, Ill.: InterVarsity Press, 1984], p. 170).

Question 8. There are two dangers in remembering what is behind: we may become complacent or we may become discouraged. In this passage Paul is probably addressing those who think they have reached a spiritual level which no longer requires that they "press on." At the same time, some people look back on the mistakes they have made and see no hope that they can persevere long enough to reach the goal.

Question 10. In this verse Paul reminds us that gifts from God to us require an active response from us. Perhaps Paul meant it as a paraphrase of Jesus' words in Luke 12:47-48.

Scott and Cindy Bunch-Hotaling live in Olathe, Kansas, where Scott is a minister of youth and Christian growth. Cindy is an associate editor for InterVarsity Press. Scott and Cindy have also coauthored two Created Male and Female Bible Studies, and Cindy authored five other guides in that series. Scott is the author of the Truthseed Bible Study 1 Timothy (Cook Communications).

What Should We Study Next?

A good place to start your study of Scripture would be with a book study. Many groups begin with a Gospel such as *Mark* (22 studies by Jim Hoover) or *John* (26 studies by Douglas Connelly). These guides are divided into two parts so that if 22 or 26 weeks seems like too much to do at once, the group can feel free to do half and take a break with another topic. Later you might want to come back to it. You might prefer to try a shorter letter. *Philippians* (9 studies by Donald Baker), *Ephesians* (13 studies by Andrew T. and Phyllis J. Le Peau) and *1 & 2 Timothy and Titus* (12 studies by Pete Sommer) are good options. If you want to vary your reading with an Old Testament book, consider *Ecclesiastes* (12 studies by Bill and Teresa Syrios) for a challenging and exciting study.

There are a number of interesting topical LifeGuide studies as well. Here are some options for filling three or four quarters of a year:

Basic Discipleship
Christian Beliefs, 12 studies by Stephen D. Eyre
Christian Character, 12 studies by Andrea Sterk & Peter Scazzero
Christian Disciplines, 12 studies by Andrea Sterk & Peter Scazzero
Evangelism, 12 studies by Rebecca Pippert & Ruth Siemens

Building Community
Christian Community, 12 studies by Rob Suggs
Fruit of the Spirit, 9 studies by Hazel Offner
Spiritual Gifts, 12 studies by Charles & Anne Hummel

Character Studies
New Testament Characters, 12 studies by Carolyn Nystrom
Old Testament Characters, 12 studies by Peter Scazzero
Old Testament Kings, 12 studies by Carolyn Nystrom
Women of the Old Testament, 12 studies by Gladys Hunt

The Trinity
Meeting God, 12 studies by J. I. Packer
Meeting Jesus, 13 studies by Leighton Ford
Meeting the Spirit, 12 studies by Douglas Connelly